Words To Love By

I0087310

Nefertari Nelson

Words To Love By
Nefertari Nelson

© 2016 Nefertari Nelson

All rights reserved. Except for use in the case of brief quotations embodied in critical articles and reviews, the reproduction or utilization of this work in whole or part in any form by any electronic, digital, mechanical or other means, now known or hereafter invented, including xerography, photocopying, scanning, recording, or any information storage or retrieval system, is forbidden without prior written permission of the author and publisher.

ISBN-13: 978-0692685938

ISBN-10: 0692685936

Published by Broken Bars Publishing

www.brokenbarspublishing.com

Printed in the U.S.A.

Dedication

This book is dedicated to my late mother Lillie Mae Nelson, and her great grand baby, (My late grand baby boy) Aidan. You are loved for all eternity.

This book is also dedicated to Octavia, Olivia, Shawn, Jr., Shawna, Shayna, Alani, and, Amir.

Read Nefertari's amazing story of survival and the quotes that she now lives by.

Words To Love By
Nefertari Nelson

It was Sunday, June 8th, 2008. Nine months into my fifth pregnancy, I was relaxing at home, watching television, when it happened.

As I rolled over to get up off my deep couch I felt a pain stronger than I had ever felt before. Since this was my fifth pregnancy I knew it wasn't labor. I rolled onto the floor but the pain disappeared and I thought it was gone for good. Although I had called the doctor, I quickly called back and said I was fine and started back to my couch. Suddenly it hit.

It was just like they had explained. It felt like a piano or an elephant sitting on my chest. I wanted nothing more than to remove it so I could get just one breath of air. Movement was around me but the next thing I remember was my husband getting me to the car and rushing me to the hospital. When I arrived the nurses quickly got me back to labor and delivery.

The doctors were puzzled. They were unable to diagnose my problem, and I was left to sit in a hospital room for hours without care. I felt every pain. Even though they gave me strong pain medication it didn't help with my inability to breathe.

The next morning did come. The man who walked in and introduced himself as a cardiologist is still, today, one of my heroes. He said he thought he knew what was going on and that he had ordered a helicopter to take me to the hospital of the University of Pennsylvania as I was in southern New Jersey. I was pretty drugged but I do remember hearing voices. The next thing I knew was in the critical care unit with hundreds of tubes and doctors surrounding me. I looked up and one of the doctors said "You are a very sick lady. You are alive but we need to decide if we are going to spare you or your baby. You and your husband have to make a decision."

I refused to decide. I could feel my baby moving and thumping around just as her four siblings before her had done. I knew I had four children at home who needed me, but how could I just spare my own life and not give this new beautiful life a chance?

This was Monday, June 9. Daily I had dozens of doctors and nurses coming in to visit the woman who actually survived a coronary artery dissection. Yes, my coronary artery had broken completely in half, and while I was left untreated the bottom front of my heart died. It was an actual heart attack. I was experiencing cardiomyopathy (enlarged heart) and the dead heart muscle was forming an aneurysm that could rupture at any moment. I was a walking time bomb. All this, and I was still nine months pregnant.

During one of my daily visits from the crews of doctors who wanted to examine "the sickest woman in the hospital" I looked to my right to see a five foot petite beautiful blue-eyed blonde storm in, as though she had been trying to reach my room for days, and announce that she is not losing me nor this baby. Not on her watch.

She introduced herself as Dr. Michal Elovitz, an attending physician in Maternal Fetal Medicine. She came close to my face, and I looked up with tears in my eyes and said, "I don't know where you came from or who you are, but I know because you are here, everything is going to be all right." She caressed my face and ordered everyone out of my room, making demands for accommodations for her to be at the hospital until the baby is delivered.

The week went on. I had several visitors. My husband sat by my side. I had the world's best nurses. I received hugs, kissed and encouragement daily. It was Saturday, June 14, my mother's birthday. She had suffered a massive stroke four years earlier and was unable to be with me due to her own disability. My coworkers were visiting when I felt a cramping at the bottom of my belly. My coworkers, working overtime to bring a smile to my face by telling inappropriate jokes, could see that I was in pain and informed my nurse.

The next thing I knew I was surrounded by at least fifteen doctors and nurses. I had been placed in a glass room with collapsible walls for just this reason. A quick and easy trip to the operating room.

When I opened my eyes I saw those same blue eyes staring at me. Her hair was in a ponytail and she had on a sweat shirt and jeans and I was able to smile as I touched her sloppy ponytail. She said "Yes, I have been sleeping here waiting for this moment and I knew it was going to be today." I had told her it was my mother's birthday. We arrived in the operating room and they set me up. She had never before delivered a baby vaginally in that operating room. We were praying that today would be the first.

As I lay there I was being pumped with blood and IV in almost every part of my arm. I was instructed not to push. At that point I was 10 centimeters dilated (the point when the baby should descend) and nothing was happening. Because I had been given so much blood my heart began to shut down and my lungs filled up with fluid. It felt like when you are swimming and you accidentally get water in your nose. I was drowning in my own fluids. Not under Dr. Elovitz's watch. She yelled something and the next thing I knew I was breathing again. She asked what kind of music I liked. I said "Jazz, but I also love club music." She said "Club music it is!" and she ordered the staff (of maybe 30 people) to play club music. She yelled "Neffie, you promised me a baby." I was told at that moment I said to her "You got it!" and I bore down and she vacuumed out a beautiful baby girl. She ordered the anesthesiologist to give me something for the pain but she made me open my eyes to identify my baby. She brought her close to my face and whispered "You did it." Barely alive, in a weak voice, I said, "We did it."

That was a rough night. I was unable to take the medicine that works for cramps and I couldn't see my baby. She was in the NCU safe and warm with the best nurses in the world. I was the one who was in critical condition. When I looked to my left I had a nurse sitting by my side and when I looked to my right the same. I was in such poor condition that I had two critical care nurses sitting two inches from my side. They told me that the next 24 hours were crucial. My buzzers beeped and alarms went off. The nurses did their jobs and I was right back each time.

As soon as I was strong enough, almost 12 hours later, I demanded to see my baby and they made it happen. What a moment it was. She looked just like my baby picture. She had a tiny IV in her arm and a blood pressure cuff on the other arm. She was so content laying there in her own private incubator. I wept thinking about all that she went through.

Days went by and we both got stronger and healthier. Although I did have a minor setback with a bout of pneumonia, I was still able to bring my baby home a week later.

Our journey was just beginning. I was going home to five children and a failing heart. To repair the dissection doctors had to place three stents in my coronary artery, which required me to take blood thinners and about nine other pills daily. The blood thinners required constant monitoring, especially in the beginning, so I had to travel to Philly every two days with five children, hardly able to walk. It was tough but I was happy to be alive, so I was happy to do it.

I found out later that my heart wasn't functioning as effectively as they had hoped so I was admitted back into the hospital so that doctors could place a defibrillator in my chest.

This is a device that shocks the heart back into rhythm should it stop or begin to beat too fast. Continuing with my positive attitude, I was thankful that such technology existed and was given the label by several doctors and nurses as the most positive patient ever!

I live today as a disabled person. Although at one point my ejection fraction (a scale that doctors use to measure heart function) was only 17 percent. (Normal ejection fraction is 50 to 70 percent) It is now up to 35 percent, which is still critical but an improvement.

I enjoy my life, don't get me wrong. It is a constant battle fighting depression and anger but I find myself being thankful for every single moment. I no longer see life as a constant struggle, but as an opportunity to make a difference. I know how it feels to be at the brink of death and I am able to tell other heart patients that no matter how bad things may look now, it will get better. I tell them to trust in whatever higher power they believe in and to accept that the future is not in their control. What shall be, will be. Enjoy the present. Life is even more precious once you've almost lost it.

I can now laugh, shop (with assistance), drive, and I am almost able to do 45 seconds of the dance, "Single Ladies" by Beyonce!!! I have learned to appreciate my medicine and value my doctors. I view the tests and appointments as opportunities to learn more about my condition so I can share with others. I try to remain positive and I smile when I look at my defibrillator scar. Not only do I think about how awesome it is that such technology exists but to live in a country that allows someone like me, a middle class mother of five, to receive such wonderful medical care is just an amazing thought that I don't take for granted.

Thank you for reading my story!

Quotes And There Meaning
According To The Author

1.

"When your words match your actions ultimately your spirit, finances and physical being will do the same."

Having a massive heart attack changed my life. I had to take a long look at myself. I saw that I smiled a lot yet with that very mouth I was able to lash out verbally if I even slightly disagreed with someone else's opinion. I had been taught that there is power in words, I knew how the Word tells us that the world was spoken into existence by our Holy Creator, however I had not realized how much damage I was doing with my words.

This quote helps me to remember to think before I speak. It also helps me to speak from a place that I have developed not from a place of emotion. I strongly believe that there is life in our words and that our words have power. I believe that the meditation of our hearts eventually comes out of our mouths, bringing our words to life. For that reason, I try to speak according to the outcome that I want to achieve, which is always a positive one.

2.

"Enjoy the moment. If at this moment the sun seems to shine brighter, sugar seems to taste sweeter, and you have a pep in our step, then do not dwell on yesterday nor worry about tomorrow, just enjoy the moment. "

When we are in our weakest of moments, it is then that we must choose to either stay down, or get up and fight. Once we have risen from that moment of weakness, we should enjoy that victory. Don't harp on the negativity that caused you to fall. Rejoice in that moment of triumph.

3.

"Never under estimate the power of
"Something told me."

Everyone has experienced that moment when they didn't run that yellow light because a little voice in your head said "DON'T." and right in front of you there is a car accident. Or that moment when that same voice whispers for you to call a friend, and that friend says to you, "I needed someone to talk to." That something is the voice of the most positive force- never take it for granted.

4.

"Judgment comes when you take
every negative thing that you know
you are capable of doing and thinking
everyone else is doing it."

In life we tend to do and believe what you've witnessed or have done in the past. If you lie a lot, you will assume everyone else also lies. If you cheat, or steal, you will also look at others as if they do the same. Those who do good things, believe that others do the same.

5.

"A person who always takes, always needs. A person who always gives, always has."

Through my years I have noticed that the people in my life who seem to always need, whether it is money, or help, never seem to offer anything to others. On the rare occasion that they do give, they feel that they should have been praised by the person or by everyone that they tell of their actions.

I've also noticed that some who work hard to get what they have, try to enhance the lives of others by sharing, and are never without. Their spirits are lighter, and they are a pleasure to be around. They are almost always in a good place financially.

6.

"Allow the wisdom that is in your heart to come alive in your actions and become an inspiration for someone else."

I believe life offers lessons that cause us to be tested in our daily routines. Our test results are determined by how much we pay attention, and by applying what we have learned from the lessons life teaches us. Use what you've learned to help someone else.

7.

"You will never get ahead by climbing on the backs of others. Eventually the person will stand up and you will be forced to stand on your own two feet."

Many people have never learned how to do for themselves. They believe using the word "You" when talking about their faults will help them justify their actions. It never does.

We must be accountable for our own lives and take responsibility for our own flaws in order to get to a place where we can stand tall. But using, blaming, or accusing others of being the reason you are not where you want to be in life, or trying to use others to get there will never end well.

8.

"When kneeling to pray, be sure to believe you are deserving of what you are asking for. If you feel you are not, work on becoming that person."

On many occasions I have heard people talk about others who are first in line to pray at church on

Sunday, yet on Monday they do not live the life that is becoming upon His sight. Those who talk about others, wonder why their lives are not fulfilled.

It is important to be who you are Monday through Sunday. None of us are perfect, but He is always watching and forgiving our mistakes. Not just on Sunday, but every day.

9.

"After reflecting, be sure to repent."

So many people are suffering from mental and emotional issues due to mistakes that they have made in the past.

Those memories may still exist, however if you truly and humbly are a better person than you were, see yourself for who you are, not who you were.

If you were a victim, and you want to be freed from the pain, ask God for help and believe that He will rescue you. Then let it go. You deserve it!

10.

"Peace is when you can close your eyes every night knowing you have done your best to do what's right."

There is no better feeling then lying in bed and smiling about who you are as a person. I remember years ago in college, I bumped into a young lady and knocked her books over. She made a scene and embarrassed me by calling me names. Later that night I laid in bed thinking about all of the mean things that I could have said to her to get her back for hurting my feelings.

Today, in the spiritual place that I am in I am proud of the young girl who just picked up her books and handed them to her. I can smile and know that I did the right thing and some of those same people that were in the room at the time are Facebook friends of mine. When they comment about me they say "You were always kind to others." Don't allow temporary negativity to change who you are. Not even for a moment. You will feel better following your gut at all times.

11.

"Serenity is deleting negative thoughts as they try to enter your mind and replacing them with a calm inner peace that is achieved when you know the love of your higher power."

I noticed when something goes wrong, such as the battery in my car dies while it's raining outside (and yes that has happened) automatically other negative thoughts try to cause me to feel bad about life as a whole.

Those thoughts try to take over and put you in a place that is dark and unhealthy. Instead of allowing that to happen, when something goes wrong I think of all of the good that has happened prior to that moment, and will happen after this one incident has passed. It was just a moment. Go to your happy place until that negative moment is over.

12.

"Love.... Believe it, Think it, exude it, receive it and foremost give it."

This is my favorite quote because I believe it best describes what others feel from me. I have been asked for years what it is about me that makes me so happy. This quote describes it best.

13.

*"Despite the good you may do, your
accomplishments and your
achievements, there are people just
sitting back waiting for you to make
one mistake so that they can shine a
bright light one it. Don't let them get
you down. You are a product of the
ultimate light. Keep shining and
moving forward."*

We all know we can't please all
of the people all of the time and in
fact some you will never please.
Allow your inner light to guide you
during the dark times.

Jealousy is a human emotion.
It's natural to feel jealous. However it
should be used to help improve or
move you in a direction that is
positive. If your feelings make you
feel the need to hold someone down,
insult their efforts, or destroy what
they are building, then jealousy has

turned to envy which is evil energy and needs to be released.

A healthy dose of jealousy lives in all of us since the beginning of time. It's a defense mechanism which makes you guard and defend what's yours and it may even cause you to try a little harder if you see someone doing just a little more then you are doing. Just be sure it doesn't make you think or have evil thoughts. That is no longer jealousy that's envy.

14.

"Be careful who you share your personal and intimate thoughts with. They may be waiting to use them against you. Know the difference between honesty and malicious intent."

Avoid people who constantly feel the need to take a side shot at you or hurt your feelings. You don't need that negative energy.

29

Instead, surround yourself with people who encourage and uplift you, as well as who support your ideas. You will see a noticeable difference in yourself when you have a positive circle of people around you.

15.

"We can't live our lives hoping others will treat us the way we deserve to be treated. We can only live our lives treating others the way we would like them to treat us."

You can only change you, how you feel, how you view things that you have been through, what you do with the lessons you've learned, and how you move forward after adversity. You can't wait on others to tell you or treat you like you deserve. You must make that happen for yourself.

16.

"The moment you are not doing what is pleasing to God, you are doing the opposite."

Your gut know right from wrong. Even if you don't remember exact quotes from the word or even what you've been taught though out your life. At every given moment you have a choice you will either choose good or evil. Be mindful whose side who want to be on.

17.

"There is good and there is evil. You can't be both."

Many times people try to fit in with those around them. You can't fit in with the evil minded if you are genuinely good at heart.

18.

*"Procrastination today leads
to tomorrow's regrets."*

Get it done NOW! Not
tomorrow, not next week. NOW! You
are not promised tomorrow.

19.

*"For every ten people who love you
there will be one who hates you for no
apparent reason. Accept the things
you cannot change and continue to be
your best you"*

Some people will get stuck on
that one person at work, or that one
family member that just likes to be
confrontational. Sometimes that's a
hidden admiration. Keep being you.
They will either climb or board and
ride with you, or flee away from you.

20.

"Earn their trust by living your best. Once that trust is earned they will come. That's when it's time to tell them about your trials and tribulations. Once they see that your walk has not been easy, they will want to know more. That's when you tell them how great God is."

I very rarely mention my belief system before a person asks. I live a certain way and if it's attractive to others they will ask and I will share the secret behind my smile.

21.

"We all go through trials and tribulations. To do so is human but it's what we do during and after our tribulations that defines who we are. Allow what you have been through to weave you into a better version of who you were. Like a butterfly in a cocoon (chrysalis) come out and

spread your wings not to be boastful but to display the beauty that comes after the storm."

I suffered a life changing heart attack in 2008. I think I have told that story a million times. It's not to brag or boast but to share my experience. It is my hope that someone will learn in some way by what I have been through and see how I turned such a negative experience into such a positive outcome!

22.

"Our truths are what help us develop our resilience. It's in those same truths that should help you mean what you say, and what you think when you pray."

So many times we walk this earth as empty vessels, just surviving. Trust me, I have been there. Don't block out your reality. Face it. If it's not what you want it to be, change it.

If you are thankful for it give thanks to God and tell another how you achieved it. If you don't face your truths, you will see them again and again until you face them head on. But you don't have to do it alone.

23.

"When your words match your actions ultimately your spirit, finances and physical being will do the same."

It's my mantra. Mean what you say and say what you mean. This is a tried and true method and key to success spiritually, emotionally, and financially. If you do this everything else will fall into place.

24.

"Enjoy the moment. It's in this moment that the Sun shines brightest, sugar seems sweeter, and you have pep in your step. Don't worry about tomorrow, just enjoy the moment."

Worry has never led to anything good. Do your very best moment by moment and you will love your outcome.

25.

"There are not a lot of things that we can believe in without questioning. Love is one of them. Hold it in your heart and allow it to bud and grow until it becomes who you are.

There are many forms of love. Each of them are powerful. Allow yourself to love and be loved, and you will have many experiences that will have an impact on your life. We are created with love. For that reason, live, love, and be loved.

26.

The strongest force in the universe is love. Allow yourself to be on the team that will always win."

When a person feels the need to make hurtful jabs towards you it's because they are unhappy within. "Hurt people, hurt people."

27.

"Don't kill them with kindness. That's sarcasm and not sincere. Live your life the best that you can. Your inner love and happiness will guide them if they truly want change."

You were created to be you. There is no one who can be you better than you. What you can do is shine your light so that the world will see what God has given us. Your shining light will inspire those around you.

28.

"If you don't make a deposit don't expect anything to be available when it's time for a withdrawal."

So many times we will do for others, giving, sharing, and investing in them. Remember to take the time to refuel your mind, body, and soul. You must be your number one priority.

29.

"God will give you step by step instructions on how to love your spouse, children, friends, and family."

God not only gives us the loved ones, He teaches us how to love them. Follow the Word, your gut and you will get your answers concerning those you love the most.

30.

"If your self-worth is defined by the opinion of your oppressor you will never love yourself."

Delete everything negative that you have learned about who you should be what the majority of people like you are doing, and how hard it will be if you want to change. Those are emotional shackles. Break the shackles and be whoever or whatever you want to be.

There is a time to look at things and walk away as there is a time to stop and look into them

31.

"Your gut is always right. You will know don't let thoughts or emotions get in the way."

When you know in your gut you are being tested, don't stop until you pass the test. If you stop what you are supposed to be doing, you will be tested again.

My oldest daughter learned this the hard way. After the fourth time doing the same thing, she finally says "Maybe I should do things differently." and she got different results.

32.

"Lead by example."

It seems that some guys take pride in the number of women they have had one night stands with, they had toyed with, or have left crying, yet when they are ready to settle down they want a women who is not damaged. Ironic isn't it?

33.

"Be careful. Sometimes there is a snake in the garden that you can't see. Be still and just listen. Many times it will leave on its own."

I have learned that my spirit will whisper which is my cue to slow down and just watch to see what my next move should be. The wrong move can be very detrimental in some situations

34.

"Remember when a friend in going through tough times that it is not your burden to bare. Be a friend, listen and love, but don't let them use you as their punching bag. You were not the problem make that clear to them."

A friend loves, hugs, and supports but do not allow that friend to transfer their negative energy onto you. Instead, remain positive, and even project that positivity onto them.

www.ingramcontent.com/pod-product-compliance
Lightning Source LLC
Chambersburg PA
CBHW071448040426
42445CB00012BA/1482